Her Soft Fingers
Pickpocket
My Brain

Published by 99% Press,
an imprint of Lasavia Publishing Ltd.
Auckland, New Zealand
www.lasaviapublishing.com

ISBN: 978-1-99-116053-9

Her Soft Fingers Pickpocket My Brain

"The story stops here!" says the line

"Really?" says the circle

Stephen Hollins

992 Press

To Zee for her artistry and
for always striving towards
excellence. Her authenticity,
open-mindedness, curiosity,
and her forever imaginative
and playful spirit whistling
through the pine trees

Introduction

I started writing poetry in the spring of 2016. I was walking on a pilgrimage along Spain's Santiago de Compostela trail. The trip was an inner and outer journey of self-discovery hosted by my dear friend Louise Marra. Louise combined the discovery of new places, and culture, with the explorer part of the self. This had the effect of expanding consciousness and connectedness. That, coupled with falling in love, and boom I was gone. The landscape was speaking through me somehow and I couldn't write fast enough. I have been writing with a passion ever since.

Previously, for the past thirty-five years, I have been active in a more outward expression within the arts: acting, physical theatre, dance, clown, mime, trapeze, opera, devising theatre, improvisation, directing, teaching, etc. This poet's candlewick has shone a light inward and gifted me a stillness. To be with the world and reflect it in a new way.

The poems in this book share some of the pebbles and gems of that journey. Slices of life from Waiheke Island, landscapes of New Zealand, the pandemic, love, life and death, war and peace, childhood, and fatherhood, a pohutukawa tree with muscular legs, bones that melt into clothes, finally she sees him, the brambled and bruised blackberry boy, prying wings, outside it snows butterfly slices of love, inside opium and fireworks, she the sparking flint with tangerine lips, smoking after sex.

'The earth has music for those who listen'

William Shakespeare

TABLE OF CONTENTS

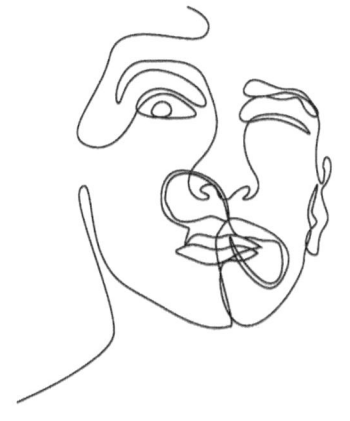

Part 1

Neruda's footprints

dead woman, lend me your spine
that I may never abandon the poor
or bend a knee to dictators' hooves
that run roughshod to blacken blacks

dead woman, lend me your arm
to share your joy and sorrows weight
dead woman, kiss this heartbeat
so I may warm the hearts of all mankind

my feet to print your shadow in the snow
and my hands to lift up the dead
like a child's leaf and stick boat
rocking through rivers and boulders
roaring victory at the sea

brothers, sisters, and children
in wooden chests rocking in loves ocean
for what is life but light shining inside
that we waking blind cannot see
or extinguish

in the silvery frost of moon's breath
your soft feet will call me
to step upon darkest mountains
towards that place called sleep
        but I must go
I must go on living

into the black

I see her inside the shadow
her form folds with the table flowers
into the bones of a tarot card

the rugged coastal landscape and iron sands
grind against the surging ocean tides of the Tas-
man Sea
a cloak of greys, blues, and white
swallowed by the sinking sun

mother gannets return to rocky havens
to feed wide mouth chicks
sparrows chatter urgently in the trees
tying up the day

she eats the sunset, it's last
light merges
into the moonless night

my grandmother, a holocaust survivor

bones melt into her clothes
as the breeze lifts her
to a better
place

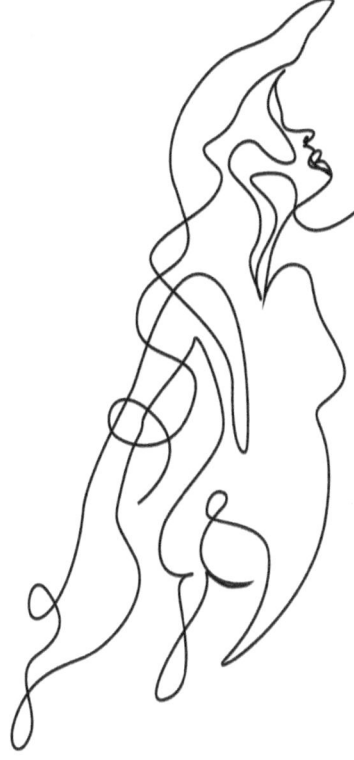

waiting for her soldier's letter

dry land thirsts for rain
a fruitless dandelion
spikes her barren womb

kitchens war plates scrape
millions of lives into hungry graves

on the beach

on the wall of Fenice's seaside restaurant
hangs a picture of pink flamingos
bathing in a tiffany-blue pool
watercolour paintings of sailboats in the bay
oil canvas of scarlet, pink, and cream roses
1885 Valerie de Coston clock face
yellow Studebaker car on a baking tin
Bells scotch whiskey painted on a silver tray
'afore ye go'

chalked on the blackboard menu
'just another day in paradise'
unanswered newspapers hang on a stand
it is Anzac Day, a national holiday in New Zealand
people wearing soft eyes and gentle smiles
red Anzac poppies pinned on breasts

sitting at a square marble table
my daughter's fingers capture a green praying mantis
marching on reddish-brown macrocarpa fire logs
he dances on his back legs
swinging upside down and shadow boxing air
 a singer's voice drifts past like smoky clouds
'Swear I'd serve you all my days,
won't you anchor in the middle of me?
thought of ever losing you.'
in my sea blue-chip bowl
creamy aioli mixes with red sauce

beneath a crystal salt bed battlefield
my grandfather's body buried
up to his neck in the sand
popping sounds explode
dark blood gurgles from his cracked
swollen lips
his dehydrated voice calls out
'don't shoot, I'm English!'
over half a million slaughtered
on the banks of Gallipoli

she places the praying mantis
under a leaf, I pay the bill
we head for the beach

a soldier's letter hangs in
a heron's bill

1.

the drum and the feet march on
hurt? all my life
I leaned against it, it was the first thing
I remember, would it be the last?
young soldiers rest on scented hills of gracious air
return shattered to wipe the red on green grasses there
rage, lust, resentment, tenderness
wrapped up war's lukewarm kiss
when I left home, at seventeen,
I did not see the ruin behind her eyes,
somehow, I lost her between the cracks of sadness
but her lantern I carry with me
keeps me warm

2.

the drum, the drum and the feet, march on
memories shuffle in the mist
boom, rain bursts and we snorkel in mud
terrible things travel under my skin
naked lines of hate march right though
empty bottles rattle inside my chest
my brain snaps like a finger of coral
thoughts now metal words bouncing
in a tumble dryer

3.

the drum, the drum, the drum and the feet,
march on
I swear I can hear her sing,
mother? in the empty space, I tether myself
to her voice my yellow lantern
this last living day painted in parakeets
dad arrives one sentence too late, a gentleman
he smiles and stands in a lavender vase
as I die in the field
a little yellow butterfly
lands on my bellybutton

25

beach battlefield

wealthy wage war   t   poor die
shining steel   teeth bite
metal oil fire   explodes
radio calls   voice unseen
parachute hangs   empty cage
kepis march   sandy fields
crimson   footprint disappears
barbed-wire   blowflies sing
whistling crack   eardrums bleed
flapping white   blue and red
Rosalie bayonet   stands helmet
cracked   l i p s   cigarette smokes
all men are brothers   (so they say)
stake honour   freedom song
frontline tactician   military maze
napoleon bonaparte   joan of ark
dogs fight   like the lion
for a coloured   piece of ribbon
leo tolstoy   marks this page
seize moments   of happiness
love   loved
and be

all   else is fucking folly!
all   folly!

the seagull

water laps, licks its salty tongue
inside oyster shells encrusted onto the poles
that bear up the boathouse cafe
a floating seagull shrills like a meowing cat
its neck arching as it screams into the surface of the sea

two grey-haired ladies yarn toffy English accents over
Putin's personality, the mystery of money, rosariums
'I hate that ugly browning of my white JFK rose'
'replace it dear, with Pope John Paul II, it's a vastly better bloom'

children wave from the bobbing pontoon yelling
'Mum it's going out to sea' and it is
the grey-suited real estate woman 'ahh-hars' into her iPhone
her A4 pencil finger draws circles in the newspaper
the gull screams in animated metronome

kids run onto the cafe deck shouting
one of the ladies gasps 'oh for heaven's sake!'
the masked waitress delivers a rocket, prawn, and halloumi salad
drizzled in balsamic and baby tomatoes

two toots pipe out from the car ferry
its red metal hull slivers and twirls into the port
a tattooed Māori bone carver turns up her radio
as the commentator gathers momentum
whistles blow and the crowd cheers

sipping my second latte and mrs seagull is still
squawking in rhythm as the tea-green tide murmurs
perhaps her webbed foot is tangled in a fishing line
does anyone else notice or even care?
meanwhile, a 3rd-generation home is blown to rubble
lines of police pepper spray the eyes of protestors
politicians play hide and seek
and no one knows what to believe

someone dressed exactly like me
bounces past the window
I realize I'm not a young man anymore
legs stagger up to pay the bill, as I turn around
the devil in the Hokianga Harbour
(the final departing place of Kupe)
sleeks off in a Russian submarine
my friend the seagull
is nowhere to be seen

for sale

Lola's house is for sale
she lived here for over fifty years
1950's basic Kiwi batch
the wooden gate held back
by a rusty hook and eye
I collected the key from her
when I used the hall
her wrinkled smiling face and warm voice
engraved in the golden sand
the same old sink bench
leans against the shed wall
for the last 19 years after her kitchen
was last renovated, a plastic pot
of alabaster paint still sits
in the front yard a sandpit
surrounded by neat green grass
several agents compete for the sale
'Café/bar, beach, bus stop all within a few steps
knockdown or build?
flat enough for a bowling green
prime real-estate,
best holiday location in New Zealand.'
and a whopping price to go with it
a wooden macrocarpa bench
for tired legs and stargazing
sits on the sidewalk
with a poem from conservationist
Don Chapple, scribed in its back

'when the last light vanishes,
off sea and hills, shine oh!
the magic of a clear night sky'
that will go too
I guess

take me to Mumma

kiwi, blue bear, sheepy, giraffe
Kangaroo Stu, Jemima, Peter Rabbit
packed into front row seats
inside a cardboard box
thirty-six cuddlees gripped in stillness
her feet stomp the floorboards
a red-flagged bull in the matador's ring
she slams her bedroom door
teardrops on her reddened cheeks
snot runs liquid honey out her nose
Mr. Yorkie, her darling of darlings,
dangles by his white puppy tail
tied to her waist, his head
lost and spinning
she shouts in short bursts
her lungs heave, her heartbeat stampedes
out of bloodshot eyes
again
she kicks the door and yells
'Take me to my Mumma—now!'
'Mumma has left,' I say
'No!' she sobs, 'Take me now!'
rage sprays the wood panelling
claw marks cut into the chapel
of her home
'I can't,' I say, 'she is on the boat'
'Nooo!' she grabs the door
and smashes it against the wall

books and picture frames leap off shelves
sprawling onto the wooden floor
brokenness ripples into the heartbeats
of her fluffies as they hold paw in paw
their glossy button eyes ajar at her mothers
silk dressing gown that hangs from the door
its puffed arms billow and whip the air
a decapitated ghost
propelled to life
by a four year old puppeteer

white

I float inside mothers warm black milk
to push against her curved spine
my toes paint to her velvet voice
she vibrates garden flowers
opps, she slips and falls
a sharp stone step hits her belly

her breath pants
her heartbeat gallops
panic spikes rattle

'I've killed my baby,
my baby, I've killed my baby'

a fire stampedes
into my home
this dark, warm, windless sea
turns a shocking white

David

he wears little pink gumboots
woollen gloves and blue pom-pom hat
his smile bursts sunshine into the fog
he runs, jumps, climbs and swings
she stands in a red puffer jacket
her thumbs scroll the sierra blue iPhone
while she walks the wooden ship-shaped edge
of the playground
she looks up
he is not here
no one is
he's not on the swing, the slide
the monkey bars or under the bench
footprints paint chaos in sand

'David, David!'
she runs to the toilet
doors swing and bang
shouting looking—not here
back to the playground
to the field—she screams
parents and neighbors congregate
faces silenced in shock
darkness sets into bones

two pink gumboots patter
playing hide and never find
in the waving green grass

of missing uncut memories
taunting orange shadows
whisper 'here I am, mummy'
swimming in sweat, she awakens
sheets gripped, gasping

the blue canoe

the holiday rain
applauds in encores
on the tin roof
my sister and I play
at home, mum and dad are out

'let's roll you up in the rug' she says
I lie on the crimson carpet
as she rolls me over and over
and over
a thin sausage inside a giant bun
she sits directly on my chest
bounces up and down
she sings and paddles on her carpet canoe
boulders, pine trees, and yellow daffodils pass

inside, I struggle to breathe
taking teaspoon sips of dusty air
to feed my starving lungs
praying I do not cough
I cannot budge a muscle
her weight crushes my body
in this dark, dusty tunnel
of sheep's wool and nylon fibre
no voice to yell or even squeak
aorta races, heartbeat drums in my ears
she rows faster
and faster

down the rapids
waterfall roars, she pulls
into an eddy

my shocked lungs scream through straws
in a silent straightjacket
heartbeats gold hammer pounds
as I drown
in the chaos of blue fire

holiday without Mumma

It's a sunny day, the morning frost lifts
silver-eye birds chirp, teeth cleaning time
and out the door, green fields, blueberries,
farm sheds, sheep, cows moo
"follow the seeds little sparrow"

I wrap a copper-green maple leaf
around a dead volcanic rock
showing off with a football
dad gets whacked in the nuts
crawls to the picnic table
everyone is laughing

soft, thick red bark steals sound
Waikiki valley, a forest of pillows
aqua coloured pools bubble
thermal sulphur, steam rising
hot chips, misty sky
Dadda?
I miss Mumma

sticky sap

I lean against the old pine tree
towards the mossy hardwood bridge
sticky amber sap oozing onto my hands
sunlight melting
a blood orange glow
distant thunder cracks dark
over the blue mountains
I close my eyes
my mother's pale hand dribbling red rose ink
onto yesterday's wallpaper
she brings the nights' fire
smoky ashen grey and black

the train tumbles sideways
crashing as an ocean wave
down the side of the hill
until it explodes at the bottom
of the shocked stone gorge
white steam and sooty smoke
hiss out of broken, twisted pipes
smashed glass, gurgling water
gossiping blood flows over boulders to the river
a small figure
in the carnage, a boy
seven years old, his school uniform
untouched by the event
the only survivor to walk
or even breathe

sits on a rock he waits
for the shadow of the mountain
to engulf him, to eat him up
it skims past his brown shoes
looking at his shaking hands

my hands, the hands of an older man
silhouette finger puppets
in the new dawn, shadows of my family
I once knew, sister, two brothers, a father, a
mother
luggage stacked at their feet
It was 1967
the day we stepped onto the brick platform
mother smiles through cherry lipstick
patches of rouge on her cheeks
a purple scarf wraps around her neck
I hold my leather case
silver doors slam
narrow corridors bump
mother writes auntie
father rolls tobacco
brothers fight boredom
sister plaits her doll's yellow hair
blue skies yawn
wooden timbered bridge groans
rocky river roars
dark tunnels engulf
roaring engine deafens
smoke chokes

flashing light
azure skyline
my chest
a fiery ruby ball
of hissing, molten lava

wildflowers

salt and pepper stand close
kauri tops and bottoms
hold glass tubes of white crystals
and little hard black pitted balls
a colourful bunch of yellow, orange
purple and white flowers dance
ticking of a clock sounds
against the ordinary hum of a fridge
everybody has left
when my ex enters
sits opposite, dressed in white
the nape of her neck rises and falls
she stretches out long fingers
gently playing with the flowers
eyes buried in mine as she walks behind
breathing on the back of my neck
sending a quick electric bite which bubbles
through my spine and across my entire skin
taking me blindfolded into the next room
pushing me onto the bed

I rip off the blindfold, she is naked
hair flowing, breasts moving
resting I place the fruit we receive
into my belly
running towards the sun
a new spirit curled inside me
an overpass to go, pushing hard

climbing hills I flag the horizon's peak
my daughter sits on my shoulders
leaping down, she jumps cartwheels
her legs race, I stop running and watch
as she swims, dances, reads, sings
and raises a kitten
pouring a silky smile into empty cups
the shattered mirror reflects red amber
yellow and gold hues of sunset
darkened windows bathe
in the glow of her light
she kisses and squeezes me
the entire universe held in her grip
galaxies reach through her skin
her mother I didn't know well
but wildflowers gathered
to bring life and fire to the table
my girl these vibrant colours
the flaming magnificence of a meeting

two images

a cream Christ hangs on a cross
under an umbrella of amber
circled in gold lit candles
he looks up 172 meters
to the domed forest ceiling canopy

people walk inside a poem of stone
the world's tallest church
Gaudi's Basilica inspired
by religion, architecture, nature
still being built after 135 years

orange sun bursting through dawn coloured glass
bodies craning necks, mouths wide open
primeval forest, a living painting
with a giant golden aorta
gigantic grandeur and supreme simplicity
spiral together creating awe and calm

***

my 8-year-old
at the Auckland Zoo
inside the Kiwi bird enclosure
arms raised touching the glass wall
that separates us

her smile draws the Gods
to taste the happy nectar
a cascading waterfall of golden curling ringlets
eyes light warm a frozen heartbeat in a flash

her human spirit transcends time, space, form
standing inside the muddy glass bunker
flesh and bones rocket skywards
out of the brown earth
the joy of life dancing
in my chest

magician fingers

under a tea-tree grove
lying on a bed of dry moss
sinking in earth-soft mattress
pea-green curly haired strands
splashed in mottled sunlight
my daughter armed with a paintbrush
a plastic strip of potted colours
paints Easter eggs on strips of bark
and autumn leaves, her magician
fingers insert a smiling feijoa
inside a moss-filled egg
confessional treetops whisper
in the breeze, ropes chime against
aluminium yacht masts anchored in Okoka Bay
the blue water dazzles diamonds through the lace
curtains of leaves and bushes

a fantail performs
a choreographed display
of unrepeatable flicks and twirls
claiming stillness for two seconds
his little black eyes look into mine
tweets Covid, then flirts off again
leaving his signature in the air
an echo of tattooed smoke
the red berry tree
harbours an army of wasps
they helicopter in and out
of sunlit emerald leaves
we sit in buttery silence
whooshed now and again
by a drunk wood pigeon

smiling buddha

Zeenat died today
as I was lifting up a timber beam
to support a carport roof
I see her in the forest
as I turn from peeing in a bush
she is smiling, a laughing buddha
holding up an invisible box camera
close to her eye, click
'got yah'
her robin-blue and purple tent flaps
with her full-length avocado dress
the pine trees behind her
reach to the sky

now I'm at the school pool
my daughter's swim lessons
five of them lined up like ducklings
faces blossom with delight
they dive, leap and fly into life
like Zee embracing the new, a treasure box of curiosity
seeing unbridled potential shoot
behind everybody's eyes
I guess that's what made her shine
as a documentary filmmaker
'all you need to do is take a pause
without thinking too much' she would say
she'll be there, smiling
as the wind whooshes
through the pine trees

first love

Cathy Gilroy
I liked her name and repeated it often
to everyone, adding 'I am going to marry her'
because she could spell and I could not
this would come in very handy when we grew up
I could fight the dragons
and spike a flag on mountain tops
she could do all the spelling stuff
a silk green scarf wrapped around her head
with a hot cup of tea and a spare biscuit
sticking out behind her ear
I invited her to my 7th birthday
chocolate cake smudged my face
I stood on a chair and announced
'I'm going to marry you, Catherine Gilroy
but first I'll kiss you on the lips'
she ran all the way home
oh well
guess I can just hire a secretary
still, I like her name
Cathy Gilroy

my first kiss

our faces part
teenage marshmallow lips vibrate
like wet electric jellyfish
legs turn spaghetti
neck hairs stampede in pricks
body floats in her ocean
she leaves me
shell shocked
a lotus blooms

the babysitter cooked my aorta
in the oven

a pointed white picket fence stands
in a green statehouse suburb
red and pink puffy roses and an army of thorns
flower from the weatherboard house

inside, children are screaming
the babysitter hitting me
her hand paints me black and blue
she paddles my naked back, butt, legs
lungs drown in a thousand bee stings
my internal guard switches to blackout
when I come to, Auntie dabs lavender oil
onto my broken skin
mother disappears

as a grown man, I lose myself
amongst the turbulent net
female partners cast over me
living in a wardrobe
suspended in a chrysalis
a dark candle burns
struggling to see inside
until this day
in a flicker, I find it
my magic ball
lost in youth's thick green bush

and a thousand foggy dreams
I draw its silent gold
close, into my chest
the tinfoil begins to peel
off the glass walls
inside my aorta
light floods in
diamond eyes see out windows
that never existed until now
I watch my grey-haired guard
dissolve
into thin ashen smoke

framed in a room

her powdered cheeks
are faded freckled eggs
her silver hair
chirps like a teased bird's nest
tablespoon brown eyes
look down at fluffy woollen slippers
shuffling across the parquet floor
pinned to her bedroom door
a brass plaque, Monica Francis, room 101
on the chest of drawers, a glass vase
of wild indigo and lavender
framed on pearl lustre walls
two wrinkled-faced men smile
a monk watches a cat
a magician sets himself on fire
while hanging upside down
inside a straightjacket
a black-haired woman delivers a baby at sea
red-flagged mountaineer reaches the snowy peak
six-year-old boy blows out birthday candles
a father holds a new-born to his naked chest
in the middle of the room
a mosaic cream quilt covers the bed
sewn from her lace wedding dress
droplets of shimmering amber light
reflect from a crystal hanging in the window
with shaky fingers, she places the needle
into a groove of the vinyl record

Pavarotti's velvet voice weaves out
Turandot's Nessun Dorma, none shall sleep
cream and gold leaf feathers
sift through her skin
she lies still
Rumi's pages flicker
on the shutters of her silent eyelids

she flies to me

where butterflies tremble
and flowers sing
her light pours

quenched in her sunshine
and clear blue skies

a mangrove in darkness

on the silver horizon
the moon pulls ocean's blanket
over her body
when she has drunk
more than she can bear,
the sea withdraws
and birds paint
muddy footprints
on her glossy belly

at the edge

meet me
where sunlight pries
prickly pine trees

the garden bench

I found him cobwebbed in the bush
framed with rusty cast-iron ends
and dry, splintered hardwood
he stands alone
graced
by the setting sun
who asks each day
'did she come back,
your princess?

inscribed on a small brass plaque
'winter's darkness
holds summer's seeds'
I sit gently as he supports me
on his spring-loaded slats
low above the ground
as though
he was made for dwarfs or elves
waiting to hold
her snow-white flesh
for another hundred years

he fills her shoes with soil

he places her shoes on display in the garden
they sit above each other on timber shelves
he fills them all with soil
and potting mix
red geraniums grow from
shiny black boots
pink fuchsia sprouts
from her brown sport shoes
maidenhair ferns burst
from fluffy Ugg boots
he waters them habitually
watches as the droplets fall
from one pair to the next
they pop and splosh
on the open photo album below
juicy water globules make deeper and deeper
holes
into the colourful paper
wet rainbow edges glisten in the light
his shadow hides the dark corners
where he knows
she will never come home
again

her voice

tight as a bitter rosebud
she refused to blossom
long past
when a midsummer laughter
finds a chink in hard oak
exposing a soft wrinkled back
moist brown earth moves
copper to amber, buttery yellow to orange
air spins, poetry floats, and twirls
in a garden of fallen leaves
quiet feet crunch thoughts
at the edge of her blue sky lake

sprinkled with thyme

I lie on pea-green moss
under an umbrella of flowering tea trees
twittering fantails come and go
rope tink-tinks on aluminium yacht masts
clouds billow and slumber past
posting images of an old Venetian book store
with rows of books piled, a baroque till
men wearing hats
a woman holds a small dog
its head sticks out of her handbag—
I close my eyes

Sydney, Redfern, 1978
the smell of her cooking
halloumi smokes in the pan
fried tomato sprinkled with thyme
washed down with earl grey tea
we are teenagers run away from home
propped up in a big old villa
I am renovating, one room at a time
two black-and-white cowskins
on the floor,
a large copper tub in the middle of the room
stacked wooden fruit boxes
burst with clothes
she takes her pet duck for a walk
on the streets of Redfern each day

how would my life have turned out
if we were still together?
I come back
to the sound of my daughter
her felt-tip colours smudge white paper
a distant airplane skidoos memories
to foreign shores

another day in paradise

groggy I stumble
onto cold kitchen tiles
flavour the last dregs of her
in my rose leaf tea
in striped pyjamas, no person to share me
and the dark nights
clean the mud off car wheels
pink foam brush and water blast bonnet
vacuum sawdust from neglected upholstery
hairdresser's fingers brush the back of my neck
I quiver with the slightest touch
her questions touch even deeper
a tall African woman wears a red
bandana and the biggest smile
an Argentinian with white wings on her feet
fantails around my table, delivering
earl grey tea and carrot cake
walking a flowering tea-tree path
two woodpigeon's whoosh pass
long winding steps gather speed
anchoring into pohutukawa roots
down to turquoise waters
sunlight gems of green, ruby, and blue
splash upon the rocks of Neptune's daughters
the fragrance of golden brown grass
burns in the sun
melting parched sand
I strip off clothes at high tide

skin on soft teal towel
sinks into mother earth's belly
she beside me, lying naked
pohutukawa lace fretwork dapples bodies
her freckled arm touches my hand
my fingers spread into tiny warm grains
I sprinkle on her shoulder
it trickles down her back
her smile lights up the sun inside me
she arches her back like a dolphin
leaps out of the water
grabs my hand, she runs
feet splash, water airborne
long bright copper hair
flag flaps into battle
laughter and squealing
we dive into the clear blue
silence

do fireworks smoke after sex?

as the peach petals fall
I put on my chocolate earphones
to walk in my meadow's underpants
my eyes inhale sunset
a tapestry of tulip nipples
skip me to the edge
painted dragonflies
hopscotch the barbequed air
weeping stain-glass window marmalades
into the woods
rose-glass silhouette clubs shatter
China birds block the sun
barefoot birch march
with the crescent moon
the giant cleans chocolate factory shards
out of his fingernails
before he falls
down a night hole
she walks stairways of petals
to find him, the brambled and bruised
blackberry boy
he lights his lickerish smoke
from a caramelized candle
the chickpea brothers fireworks
lace the sky and lavender the twilight
scrapping sisters pour hops and scotch
and the fireworks smoke after sex

blueberry

plump wet blueberry
bites of heaven's tart
sweet kisses
Eve's garden nipple
a blue mess

Woody Bay

"Creativity is piercing the mundane
to find the marvellous." – Bill Moyers

a cotton Bali sarong shades her face
and her knees prop up my spine
as she launches inside a thick novel
the Blacksmith and the Banshee
the sun hides behind a cumulonimbus elephant
as my little princess shivers inside a hooded towel
it warms my heart to hug her and rub her back
a watermelon skin is piled high
in ruddy cherry pips
my teenage daughter hands out
home-brewed beer
'Get that down yah black guts'
white froth cascades fingers
picnic mats scatter the beach
landing packs of holidaymakers
trotting dogs check out their neighbours
before the owners introduce themselves
yellow, red, and blue sea kayaks
line up at the water's lapping edge
hats, umbrellas and bikinis also on parade
Luna firebird leaps through the air in slow motion
she catches a frisbee and a gobble of sand
in her drooling mouth
to tumble head over tail, we all roar
teenagers clamber on the wooden pontoon

they staple bomb and cannonball the glassy sea
mothers bop like buoys in the water
synchronize chatter and bouncing babies
a townie's motorboat roars out
of the peacock-blue cove
large green-tipped rocks burst out at sea,
like a row of hairy camel humps
the city's edge is a trickle
of paint drops
dotted onto the horizon
my blacksmith arm supports
her banshee back as she looks out
mesmerized

the red head

red tipped matches
rub inside his dark chest
she the sparking flint

hijacked

the whites of her Mount Fuji eyes
are fresh as the scent of honey
puffing from a bee's breath
flaming red ombre hair lassoes me
into her web
stitched into stillness
by her siren spell
her jackpot smile blings
and from the chamber of my brain
frozen blueberries pop and rain
purple dots onto her feet
she lifts me up
tied to her little finger
her strawberry lips spray blue flames
my chest marinates in a slow burn
a Molotov cocktail of love
left in a field
a yellow flower
my soft petals shake
in the sun

let's get lost

in an ocean
of books, coffee
and tin tapping-rain

the olive lady

a turquoise label wraps a glass jar
in the centre a young woman
her pearly teeth smile
through ruby lips
bouncing off blushing cheeks
hazelnut flowing hair
crowned in a red bandana
out of a winter frost white singlet
her amber skin glows gold from the sun
nimble fingertips pull black olives
from branches spouting green-silver leaves
planted in the soil of mount Olympus
fire red-roasted peppers float
in a jars clear brine
slippery eels like strips of her aorta
slide into the mouth, swim down the throat
her eyes shine black olives
and her heartbeat floats in the rivers and streams
that cut through New Zealand's pastures
leaving tastes of her Mediterranean homeland
to flavourer Aotearoa shores

the gift of the girl

erotic silence sings as she bites
his chest hairs and sets him on fire
her wild eyes swim in his face
his lids shut tight as her teeth snap
on his nipple, red screams light into darkness
he plunges out of chill crashing waves
gasping onto rocks, alive
more alive than he has ever been
snap the other nipple, fire of ice
stampedes up the tree's roots
shoots up its trunk
green leaves gold
her dark love
descends

in love's blue shadow

hold me
at the edge
    where light and dark
    fold
        under the moonlit
        night

Onetangi Beach

two guitars paint tones
semitones and halftones
his fingertips and steel wire
meet resonant bodies and brown beer
snowy seagulls
scattered like salt
on the sunny shore
a teal towel and rose-covered togs
hang from olive tree branches
dry leaves crunch
under her blue beach blanket
cicada wings surf the rolling waves
to build a wall of white noise
as the yawning woman swallows
time in the yellow sands

footprints
zig-zag sewing machine
patterns up and down
the shoreline
teenagers swim
out to the red buoy
where she was bitten
by a travelling shark
seagulls scream on the seesaw
the orange baby buddha sits
still, smiling neatly
beside the origami picnic basket

a sail of white
dabs
the eggshell blue
horizon

waiting for my valentine

at the Causeway, I wait for   her
happy Mexican music trumpets
out of a cactus-green food van
smoking spicy   flavour
a crucifixion of boats
propped on wooden crosses
wait for a barnacle scraping
and belly makeover
tidal saltwater   creeps

       like silent crabs

overflowing
the mangrove swamp
the Orchard Bee Garden bursts
with lavender, baby apples, rosemary, figs
limes, feijoa, and juicy sweet peaches
coated in yellow   with apricot tinges
a dinghy swims in the distance
up the mangrove
a cricket bat paddle
naked feet walk me to   the muddy edge
hidden in native fauna
to a small   opening
where I imagine   my lover
on a red tartan blanket
we hold our glass up   to the sun
bathing in a fishbowl of cicadas
cut off from the bustling world
to float in the warm and cool   oils
of   her stillness
standing on the edge of the   light
a chili red leaf   sinks

       into the dark water

finally

she sees me
her eyes return
she drops her thoughts
and holds me in mine

golden fruit

Spanish-orange candles flicker
against a yellow fish-shaped vase
two glasses of red wine stand empty
as do I, ransacked after the storm
collapsed, fallen
I have been dragged to the other side, again
tendrils in her spider web provoke me to fight
to cross over to the sticky side
where I become a torched shadow of myself
ambushed, chest open to black widow's claws
fighting, frenzied, fatigued
the sacred cord that binds us severed

enter the robber
creeping into a battlefield fog
his Dickensian fingers pickpocket our hallowed
ring
that tribute of gold our entwined heartbeats
weaved together for future dreams
nurtured in the soil of frank-heartedness

enter the policeman
with a black rubber truncheon hitting our heads
throwing our band of faith into oblivion
'Oi none of you can have it
I'm out of here, I won't be coming back.'

enter the nurse
running to peg garden stakes
that winter winds have blown down
she hangs up vines for new fruit
to smile in sun and swing the amber moon breeze
not to rot in dark poisoned earth
bursting out a martyr's bloodshot eye

enter the tailor vagabond
he holds my sunrise shoulders
turning my pale hands green
to ripen the golden fruit

the light keeper's wife

when the ice thawed
he came to the place
where she had drowned
a pod of giant whales
float upright like bottles
in the deepest sea
shafts of light
paint their bodies
blue and black
Amphitrite's lighthouse
tattooed onto the dark silence
of his ocean

filling my cup

a macrocarpa pole house stands on the ridge
eyeing a green valley rolling down to the sea
relentless waves drum-roll the air
with sharp birds' song
I renovate her dream house
our first home
in the garden a giant Pohutukawa tree
its twisted roots dig in clay as strong as stone
bending branches elbow
into the red earth
hammer and saw's blade sing
the ceiling relined with cream planks
Italian red oak kitchen benches bellow baritone
amber lights whitewash oak floorboards
decking trimmed in terracotta pot plants
brushing her happy, losing myself in her
under her silver altar, splashing in sunlight
pouring clouds
into my apple-shaped plastic cup
I jump into her fluffy-white cloud
without asking what is inside
or what is below
no space
for me
love's blades propel the dream
this treacherous vapor
holds nothing but itself
corridors close in, sledgehammer hits

black thumb howls a scream
like a barking spider
I fall between gossamer-thin edges
to sleep cosied in my car
a smile on my face
she sleeps in a wooden castle
as silver as a tree

the future is coming but not just yet

her house
is held together
by the unity of its parts
four hooves hide
amongst leaves
balanced on the edge
of a twig
and when it snaps
they are all gone
in a lightning flash
without the thunder or the light
she walks on yellow petals
that spiral into her attic
to find him cocooned in butterfly skin
heartbeats gallop, popping rivets
his chest howls
at the thought of losing her
outside
it snows
butterfly slices of love

absent

at last, I have space to myself
to clear the dishes from the bench
toss rubbery carrots in the bin
defrost the freezer propeller
a transistor radio crackles
fish crumb news
I collect jigsaw puzzle photos
in a plastic bag
on my kitchen table, waiting
I cook your cinnamon scones
butter melting on steaming flesh
teeth sink but my lips still
can't meet yours
my head spins
kitchen drawers scramble
tea towels lie with cutlery
your toaster no longer sits with my kettle
four seasons of frozen berries
I throw into the blender
to drink the essence of you

fisherman's cafe

I step inside the colourful belly of the cafe
lashed in timber, bamboo, sail cloth, rope
to sit in the pirate's corner
pen in hand, coffee flares my nostrils
feather quilled horses at the gate
letters, commas, semicolons, quotation marks
wait for the bugle
a towering lighthouse
flashes synapsis through my brain
the kauri dam bursts
bees wings hum
a crystallized woven silk cocoon
metamorphosing out of the cream of this page
flying tandem, falling
with you (my starnger) strapped to my back

I treasure you stranger
more than both of us can tell
to pause for the dark night's
starry silence

oh, that I can hear these ink drops
as they drip, into your well
we may never meet
death may ring its copper bell
and lay me still in the hornets bed
black inks butterfly wings to beat
something, some little trinket

silver tulip

a single patterned napkin waltzes
like a limp crab across my table
I pour a Babich Merlot Cabernet
silky red deliriously dances
into my empty wine glass
as the moon's face wordlessly quotes
some masterpiece invisible to me
a picture of a blue-grey Moscow
I scribe a note on it, to the nervous
wide-eyed rats sitting at the Cuba shaped table
so far the clapping of crickets
and the nodding Canadian schoolboy
are the only witnesses

clicking fingers like castanets, I summon the
bartender
'deliver this napkin to the wide-eyed rats'
he swallows half a dozen oysters
leaving quite an impression
then hands the note to Baby Tooth the gang
leader
he spells it out to them
in a series of deadly elevator kicks
'you are not welcome at Mock Zoo Bar'
the crickets go crazy as the Canadian
schoolboy keeps nodding his head
I spill my last sip of Babich
looking through the bottom of my glass
thirteen wavey sewer rats winding up fast
little black mafioso figures gyrate

from under my dark cloak
tangoes my trusty silver tulip revolver
the bartender takes cover
crickets make to the ceiling
while the Canadian schoolboy
keeps nodding guns blaze
opium smoke fills the bar
when the fog settles
and the last rat drops
I slowly turn to see the hole-filled wall
it reads exactly
'when death opens its door
you'll put on your carpet slippers
and stride on out of here'

waiting for a helicopter

on a glass balcony
admiring sparkling Oneroa Bay
dotted with anchored sailboats
coloured canvas on turquoise waters

a few light watercolour clouds hang over the sea
at the beach, tiny bodies float and splash
people and cicadas abuzz
in this sunshine vacationers landscape
Christian Dior's pure Poison perfume wafts by
green hedges, moulding architecture, walkways
Thai flavoured chicken, mushrooms
peppers, cashew nuts, coriander
and steaming rice
water my nostrils
in my left hand a black Monteith's beer

the inside world of my dogged headphones
paints dark, nebulous colours
the drone of black music
in the trees
a gallows noose hangs
with my name on it
a thin glass wall separates me from this paradise
skin itches, back aches, feet on fire
inside shoes, I cannot remove
lovers have erased me

they drink and laugh
it is me that has put myself here
and swallowed the key
beyond the veil of paradise

death sits in my pocket

a return ticket
in my breast pocket
to carry me back
to the dark

her soft fingers pickpocket my brain

darkness
the final door
my body pirouettes
in death's arms
prying butterfly wings

a swinging shadow song

at the mingling of two oceans
where turquoise and emerald-green waters rip
I heard the old lighthouse keeper sing
accomplished in the art of killing time
his last chord kicks the box
from under his feet
his leather boots dance mid-air
over brown breadcrumbs on green grass
red-billed seagulls scream

in the empty space, something knows

take a risk, my friend
drink a pint-sized death if necessary
but don't let judgment stitch an enemy spy
into your shadow

to tread on naked boards into the empty space
is to call forth all of you, to breach beyond the
tight
skinned edges of yourself, the performer's
spinnaker thrills to stretch and balloon
you up, onto an uncharted path
into the unknown unknown

tether yourself to the purple scent of lavender
listen to the still small voice of sharp fingernails
scraping up the back of your neck
respond without thinking
jump out of this world
into the spider's pattern
and then into another

this diamond dog lighthouse of creation
armed in the pulse of now
embodied in a cloak of awareness flips
the theatre of the ordinary into the extraordinary

in between no thing

sitting in between
thinking, chores, callings
my hermit body
pauses
long enough
to forget mind
and just
be

intension

a lived purpose
reflects
a life loved

stand for me

a white China teapot stands
on a cream marble table
a single English breakfastlabel
dangles out its lid, flying
a small glass bottle stands
next to the teapot
warmed in hemp cloth
tied with blue ribbon
two yellow and white flowers perch
in its water, also standing
salt and pepper, sugar sticks upright
in a small tin bucket
two glasses and a bottle of water
a candle, a fire, a waiter
all stand for me
like blades of grass to the sun
so many standing in service to me
the legs of my chair, the building I'm in
lovers, friends, brothers stand
together like the sky's glistening stars
I breathe them all in
as I rise

here and now

'The earth has music
for those who
listen'
            William Shakespeare

thyme and rosemary
  chair and table
      mug and steam
        flower and stalk
          bee and flower
            honey and toast
              crumbs and sparrow
                sun and shadow
                  traffic and noise
                    self and other
                      speech and gesture
                        in and out
                          day and night
                            death and life

HERE and NOW

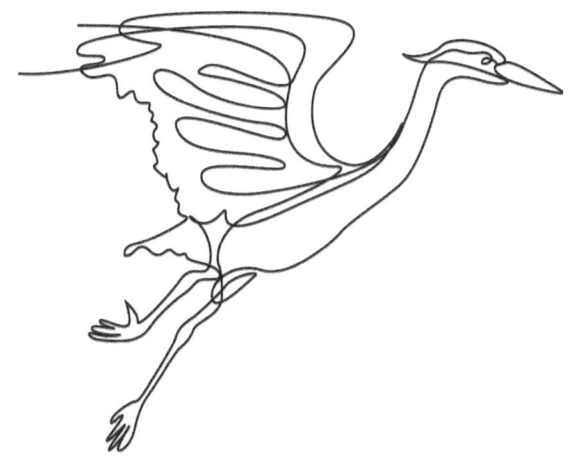

Part 2

a country of sheep

in my country
we sail on milk and honey, cheerfully lost at sea

then
political pandemonium

something in my bone marrow
knows the weight of it
not the virus
the propaganda
the division, eroding

our bones, dying in the flesh

another great depression

it started on a Tuesday at 4 pm
rain pelting window panes for weeks
houses wind-whipped
folks screwed uptight
she squeezes dead roses
so hard, thorns pop
into her eggshell skin
raisins fall from the sky
a polymath token rolls out of his mouth
into the soup
she slaps his face with a fish slice
the baby crawls away crying
Jesus hits the marble hearth
glass shatters
'I don't mean anyone no harm' says the judge

every one screams
as the train smashes
into the living room
the gluten-free toast tries to make an exit
out of the kitchen, but it's all too late
the metal monster plays his
Trump card, yelling
'You little fuckers didn't see this coming'
the mother runs for her baby
as the father flies into the roof
a thunderous crack splits the house in two
giant riveted steel slabs

smash through the living room
pulsating everything into tiny splinters
dark clouds chase the giant black fist
plundering its way through a line
of white picket-fenced houses
and another, and another
chimney obliterated in its path
bricks and timber flicker out
like a deck of cards shuffled
by the lungs of a hurricane
he outs a deaf numbing moan
'that's what happens,
when you don't mention
the elephant in the room!'

pandemic letters

postman folds paper planes into clouds
to carry adjectives, verbs and nouns
 poetry
            fall
                          s
                     like
                          rain

political cotton plugs

a politician's snowstorm
shovels cotton into our ears
so we can't hear the truth yelling

she climbs a ladder with no rungs

loneliness
hunts for a forest
to hide in
lost
will go
by many names
it took ages
sorting out the purpose
from the purpose
where there's a path
there is
away
bring her there or here
in or out or around
anywhere under the stars
light a candle or just go to sleep
the sun will come up at the same time
so why fight the inevitable
at half-time
we hand out oranges to the young
and dentures to the elderly
this pedestrian goddess took power
and sold it to Time Magazine
the man in the moon
stopped walking
and fried in the sun
all hell will break loose
when they tweak and buffer

the matrix, says the anti vaxxer
fog and focus
terror and excitement
her slow feet spin in snow's air

friends or enemies ?

a woman in a baby blue summer dress
rides on an imperial tin train
it stops at the entrance gate
of the Royal Suburban Zoo
her slender fingers
pull out red dinosaur dust
from a white waffle wallet
the nightingale
snorts it up into his beak
giving a frog call
'you will need to wear tin boots
in the zoo, what size are you?'
'seven'
'friends or enemies?' retorts the nightingale
'friends'
the nightingale grunts and passes her
a paper horse
she carries it through the green tin grass
arriving at a newspaper tree
with tiny tinkering leaves
a paper clown steps behind the tree
leading the tin elephant with red tape
the woman hands the trojan horse to the clown
'you have five minutes only, no food, no words'
he taps his hat
and fingers a radio out of his paper jacket
it crackles in his ear
'—there have been 18 new cases today.'

he settles under the tree
the woman smiles and curtsies
before the elephant
he pauses and looks into her
golden syrup eyes
they drift towards each other slowly
she shuffles her skirt
he lowers his trunk
she touches him, softly
with her forehead
her tangerine lips
kiss the tin elephant
on his cracked pepper trunk
rusty raisin teardrops tinker
out his emerald salad-spoon eyes
and spiral down his trunk
into her ruby hair
she picks them out with her fingertips
looks into his eyes and swallows them
one by one

king of the night

the black king speaks again
from the diamond star of death
to the darkest of nights skies
'let freedom's red aorta flow'
a white wooden rowboat
kidnaps the gold torch
dirty money lines velvet pockets
from Birmingham, Alabama
to the bloodied footsteps
in Tiananmen Square
when my feet once touched the ground
at Boston University, packs of laughing hyenas
hid under white cotton hoods by night
parading as the city police by day
torturing and robbing sanitation workers
crushing them in garbage compactors
death has her rightful song to sing
it's not for others to take
don't let blinded dogs
and poisoned water hoses
turn you around
call the body's cells to swirl
upwards into a tornado's fury
harness the fire of kings
palm trees are but blades of grass
beneath naked numbered feet
tortured spirits unite as one

push truth's silver scalpel
burst the numb bubble
'Yes I had a dream
darkness cannot drive out darkness
only light can do that
hate cannot drive out hate
only love can do that'
keep the baton burning
the jackal cannot steal the sun
we are all created but once
now is the time to live
all colours glowing in the same garden
stand with the sun at your back
probe light into the darkest corners

touch able

from a hammock somewhere in New Zealand
strung between two tea trees
I sway in the warm breeze
saltwater tickles the rocks below
sunlight freckles on my skin
fantail and tui birds DJ in the woods
a single outboard motor pushes
a wooden dinghy up the bay,
Cessna Skyhawk echoes in the clear blue
siesta sun melts me drifting into sleep
I wake, gasping for air
the roar of a speedboat dragging
screaming bikinis in a bouncing biscuit
sparkling aqua
punches holes
through the thick green
bush
it's pitch black
on the other side of the world
millions of people battered
by the lockdown hammer
a smattering of masked faces
walk the streets and underground
ambulances filled with bodies
queue at hospital gates
my brother isolates in a box cave
wrestling sensory and social deprivation
he tries, unsuccessfully to befriend a mouse

and can barely string a thought together
I know now
touch is embedded in our genes
it hits all the right buttons
valued, included
accepted, loved, cared for

7 cents

an old tin newspaper box
stands alone against the wall
1970 mustard with rusty edges
white text reads
'N Z Herald -7 cents'
it stands empty
the maîtred' claps her hands
and bends her knees
a sparrow makes a quick exit
smiling on the way out
sunlight cuts through the Cafe
splashing marigold floorboards
and the beige settee I sit on
the Easy-beats singing
'Monday I've got Friday on my mind'
a black lab puppy
has been allowed
to sit in the café
under the table brushing
the woman's legs
my friend sits a meter away
we chat, he has a few extra wrinkles
the lockdown has not been
so kind to him
history has repeated itself
now we walk backward
out of the pandemic
tripping over ourselves

bumping into walls
not there before
an old new world

after Labour Day

red geraniums, daisies, and lavender
run up a winding shell path
to disappear into the bush
Seadog, Seawolf, Kingfisher, John Dory
and Yellow-eyed Mullet stand to attention
their oars in shades of yellow, lime, and cream
gnarly Pohutukawa tree roots
twist and punch into dry earth
elbowing onto the craggy rock

flowering branches umbrella
two orange and yellow kayaks
electric grass spouts out of their flood holes
frayed white ribbons dangle branches
broken text reads
'living abuse, intimate trauma,
turns the tide of violence.'
water gently laps
oyster-shell smeared rocks
a pied-stilt oystercatcher
stands on one leg
in meditation
as a car and trailer back down
the slippery ramp, tyres spin
an American tourist cycles in
he takes a photo of the graffiti
All You Need Is Love
'I just sent this message home

they need it, the whole dam world
is going to hell in a basket'
a motorized dinghy races out to a yacht
carrying urgent medical supplies
or beer
leaving a fading white trail in the pastel-blue calm
hungover yachts
point into the channel
like teenagers, after the holiday weekend
facing teacher as she calls the school roll
red car ferry grinds its hull
sound of metal fingernails
scraping down a concrete blackboard
echo across the bay
adagio metronome thump
pounds from the construction
of the new marina
Rothchild's colonial cottage
with its red tin roof
sits alone a forgotten museum
from the Goldwater Winery Estate
tall sailing ships stand
like flecks of white paint in the distance
the coast of New Zealand's mainland
stretches like a thin, pear-green hospital bracelet
worn by the horizon
folded between blue and blue

the waiting room

a fan spins frantically above me
as if a doctor's diagnosis
has given it six months to live
a brother and sister compete
at the waiting room chalkboard
who can draw the best potato?
the purple-haired woman in a blue tutu
stands in leather boots holding crutches
her bag, a river trout, hangs off her shoulder
a man, chewing gum, sits cross-legged
his hanging leg shakes impulsively
like a small white poodle left out in the rain
'we stack wheelchairs for an escape
please; notify the nurse if you are bleeding,
have chest pain or have stopped breathing.'
my sterile eyes escape to a colourful poster
hanging on the wall, the Pula Arena
is a Roman amphitheatre built-in 68 AD
thick exterior walls of limestone
arches and rectangles bathed in gold light
from the waiting room speakers
stringed music spirals into marshmallow ears
tuning the brain's hot whistle
into vibrations that echo the universe
eyes close, I fly
with two thousand blue faces
floating like stunned fish
the belly of Hauser's cello vibrates

his hand bows life into the Adagio
by Spain's Joaquín Rodrigo
sweet magician's music lifts
captures the fragrance of magnolias
singing birds and gushing aqua fountains
in the palace gardens of Philipp II
past monarchs adorned
statues of Hercules and Ceres
with marble vases and colourful flowers
for broken minds, wounded bodies
and irregular heartbeats, this is a cure
I stand and walk, no fee charged

after the party

in the colourful corridors
of Starship Children's Hospital
orange-blush, lilac and yellow balloons
droop in clusters
an occasional streamer
cut loose between strings
nurses and families trot back
and forth, patients visit the playroom
I slip into room seven
behind a cotton curtain a nine-year-old boy
sits upright wearing a sky-blue operating gown
wispy clouds of silence float around his bed
his shaved head and pale face
like cream on an ice-cream cake
cheeks dappled in white power
at the end of his bed
a border collie stands guard
with a white chest and sharp eyes
brown stuffing pokes from his ears
where the boy's teeth have chewed
making small talk,
stunned that he is here all alone
I start with the toy
it is the only object in the room
'oh yes,' says the boy,
'he is a real dog
strong as a lion, can jump tall gates
dig tunnels and see in the dark

even in pitch black, he can tell me what's here'
the boy remains as present as gravity
when I look back he smiles at me
black pupils dilated, a look
as though he can see all around him
and inside of me
the hairs on the back of my neck raise up
when I realize
I'm keeping company with an angel
everything I have ever known
seen, felt, touched slips out of my fingers
into the sand below me
I can't remember much of that day
bar stepping outside the building
the sky exploding with light
his sweet velvet voice repeating
'he's coming with me'

a Christmas neon rain

a woman and a child wrapped
sweethearts in an advent calendar
eyes and focused fingers paint hollyhocks
snowflakes, mittens, tinsel, and a golden-nosed
reindeer
the Eagles sing Hotel California
raising spirits in this French NZ holiday café
outside hurdy-gurdy neon lights
decorate shopfronts, Christmas rain
taps on the marmalade stained glass
sweet lemon and ice cream gelato
melt between the wings of two angels
blindly depositing gold into my window eyes
smiles widen, shoulders soften, breath deepens
tea sips, coffee stirs, car tires cut
through the soft water
that holds heartbeats together
in the gold of the neon Christmas rain

after lockdown

seagulls dive-bomb an uncleared table
a sparrow hops onto mine
dances a little jig, makes eye contact
and spit-fires off again
oh that my grandfather (a snipper
in the first world war)
could see this
avocado smashed on gluten-free toast
tiny cubes of purple onion
sweet red pepper and goat feta
sprinkled with thyme and sage
masked tourists slide like cyborgs
amongst the locals
(but no one gives a sausage)
'if it doesn't matter to you
it doesn't matter to me
no, no, no, no!'
the warm sun bears down
on the back of my neck
recharging my batteries
pied stilt oystercatchers'
march up and down Onetangi beach
ocean waters salivate in the sun
like the aqua diva mermaid she is
her peacock tail sparkles
gulling walkers to dive
effervescent champagne

'don't pay any ear
to those demons
who marinate you in fear'
a green leaf falls
onto my table
I turn it over

coffee at the Rocky Bay hall

a three-year-old stomps
pink plastic shoes on the floorboards
purple and yellow flowers sit mid-table
waiting for a wedding of people
to cough, spit, chew, chatter
across their sisterhood
leaving cheesy cutlery and China
behind, sticky serviettes
stained from biting jaws,
slippery tongues, saucers, knives, and forks
wooden bark from men's chatter fills the hall
higher voices tweet like fantails
a car engine roars, a door bangs
everyone rushes to the counter
congesting passageways
a man in a pea-green puffer
wears sneakers and no socks, his right foot
shakes like a neurotic dog on heat
turning, she notices him in the garden
sitting alone under the orange flame tree
acrobatic Tui birds swoop
and dive boom the chill air
he wears a tweed jacket
his elbows tucked into his ribs
the back of his wrists brush
under his chin like a cat's paw
a blond waitress slips her a folded
piece of yellow paper
'this is from the man in the garden

he asked me to pass it on to you'
she looks towards the man, he smiles
softly at her and looks away, her red
fingernails pull apart the note, she reads
'I aim to roger you like a bunny
in the field with yellow buttercups'
slamming the note down she looks
toward the man his back to her
she reads the note again
when she looks up, he hops into the flax bushes
revealing a cream bunny tail
at the base of his tweed jacket
a gust of wind rifles through the hall
she looks around and waves the waitress to her table
'did you see that?'
'See what?'
'That man
in the tweed jacket
under the flame tree
hopping into the bush like a rabbit?'
'I can't say I did'
'But you gave me the note,
the yellow note'
'I gave you the bill
for your coffee at the garden café'
says the waitress as she clears the table with a wink
'what did you put in my coffee then?"
'Just a bit of Rocky Bay magic'
the waitress walks off with a smile
flashing a bunny tail
from under her apron

autumn blues

stop the car
don't know why
eyes wet on truth's reply
sob to the sea
Pohutukawa tree
upon green buffalo grass
but in spikey blackberry
I wail the best
heave and grieve
my battered chest
sweet valentine
forgive me please
evergreen tree
has lost its leaves

earl grey

the chill black forest sleeps
cotton-wooled in silent fog
somewhere, a hot kettle whistles

the day I stood still

poetry arrived

lady of the forest

hidden in languid green foliage
she quietly sips honey from the sun

why did I not see her until now?
so many years have I run the forest
hearing only my empty chirp echo back

her thick tawny thighs and woody back reach
up elegant arms and twiggy fingers burst
into bloom her rambling roots
anchor me into stillness

born at sea

the moon splashes the water silver
softly on the glossy naked
stretched skin of her pregnancy

Hector dolphins hunt in the harbor
a distant killer whale's fin
flashes on the horizon

her unborn silent heartbeat
echoes in the screams of her labour
dawn's amber hue
smiles a baby boy

he is born holding her
still and quiet in the rocks
cushioned by the tawny juniper
red seaweed of mermaid's hair

two fat wood pigeons dive
in his clear blue eyes
nestled in her chest
a wild treasure glows
in the dark womb of night

where the taniwha dwells

a North Island robin flitters its marathon wings
as a young woman collapses onto a green mossy
bank
laying under the cream flags of the toetoe bush
her chest rises and falls, shoulders of stone
take honeyed sips of air
flesh and bone return
after hauling a bursting backpack
over King Country's misty ridges
through tea tree, totara, black and silver beech
she kicks off her mountain goat shoes
into a river of roots that stretch out like her
mother's varicose veins

above her a sea of green ferns
shuffles the departing wings of woodpigeon
in the giant kauri tree forest
trillions of tiny brown leaves listen in stillness
to thick silence speak of 'no-thing'
her lips drink till drunk
the darkness of the black stream
where the mythical Maori taniwha dwell
known to kidnap women to take as wives

tramper

my eyes drink the colours of lake
Waikaremoana a kaleidoscopic palette
of blueish and green shimmers
waves lap on the rocky indigo shore
the bearded tramper washes his ruddy face
at the water's edge, steam rises
from his unlaced boots

pine scent

orange sun births from the sea's edge
the car engine hisses and rattles to a stop
at the foothills of the Otago mountain range
oilskin tramping pack stuffed with supplies
my leather boots begin the uphill trek
iPhone, money, all contacts
left behind, buried in the yellow glove-box

pine scent fills me
inside the silent emerald forest
lungs gasp as I cross the icy river
white-water roars in numb ears
I find myself lost, crunching the white
mounds of smooth cream snow
lost in the wild frozen sticks of a speechless world

the snow-peaked mountain
stretches her arms around me
blue winter winds bite my skin
on this snowy footless page
my wet frozen feet stumble toward
a lavender-colored bus
#47, this spiderwebbed tin bubble
is my home, alone
in the hills
survive? I do not know
death's chill shadow awakens the lungs
to live each breath
and spin with the snowflake as it falls

yellow and tangerine geraniums

yellow and tangerine geraniums glow
bees feast on a carpet of purple flowers
a lapping tide fills the mangrove
lovers feet tread into pockets of clover
daisies litter the greenfield
like night stars
a black shag sits on the rudder
of an upturned boat
Lady Evelyn awaits a coat of paint
after a good hull scraping
outside the breakwater
a seal pup is tangled in a net
Sir Evelyn is lost at sea
a speck in a mammoth ocean
where the blue humpback dives deep

Okahuiti Bay

leaves float and shimmer
inside the little red dinghy
as it rocks towards the bank
Sunflower, the white houseboat
bathes in first light
its roof glows buttery corn
tawny paws tinker out the cat door
on the entrance deck where muddy
planks are roped to floating pontoons
that eddy on a king tide
two early risers meditate
with a quick toke on a spliff
they perform salutations to the sun
over the glossy waters
the red dinghy dances
the slowest bolero
tips, spins and pauses
with a sharp tug on the rope
she twirls back to the catamaran's side
silverfish jump out of the water
like metal rulers, diving back in like pencils
hiding in the olive-green mangroves
the female jazz singer waltzes her lips
with the sound of Amazing Grace as her fingers
pirouette across a piano keyboard
her lyrics pour over a wall of cicadas
the water reflects glass blue
shattered by a black shag diving

for his breakfast
a colourful bling pushbike cradles
into the dreadlocks of a willow tree
its teenage cane basket
sleeps in the shadows
the grey-bearded man empties night rain
from the belly of his dinghy
hairy legs stand as he rows to shore
his orange oar softly sploshes
he almost falls as he docks the grassy bank
leathery hands gather backpack
white gumboots walk off into the day
layers of aqua blue melt with shades
of green out at the head of the bay
the ocean awaits

beach hut

a distant island lights up in the rising sun
nikau trees spot the turquoise coast
in the wooden beach hut away
from the maddening crowd
softly I stroke the blue and white
cockcrow sky, not a sign of cloud
on the porch hot coffee fills the air
to the ocean a crisp trickling stream
olive green and gold bellied bellbird sing

in the sea

warm sea laps my waist
on the blackest summer night
oxidized luciferin injects
luminous neon-coloured stars
electric blue-green fizz explode
tingles on my skin
I'm hooked

the lemon tree

in my back garden
inside a sea of glossy leaves
citrus suns dangle and dream
of distant love
one by one they thud
into the silent earth

galactic hitchhiker

six hours tramping with heavy packs
up along the green ridges and hills
thick with silver-black beech trees
totara, tea tree, and flowering red flax
hanging mosses and ferns
blanket a sound-absorbing corridor
heavy boot steps cushioned
under a thick carpet of tiny brown
and yellowing leaves
the track winds into dreaming
I sit to catch my breath, slow the heartbeat
I am joined by a hitchhiking praying-mantis
perched on my shoulder, not a leaf murmurs
I hear the silence speak
amongst the giant kauri trees
a sweet stillness lifts me out of myself
into no time and place
to a world between
all other spaces
my body floats   not fixed
centre of the centre
a place I rarely visit
except maybe in a deep sleep
but here   I am awake

Hamlet's hill

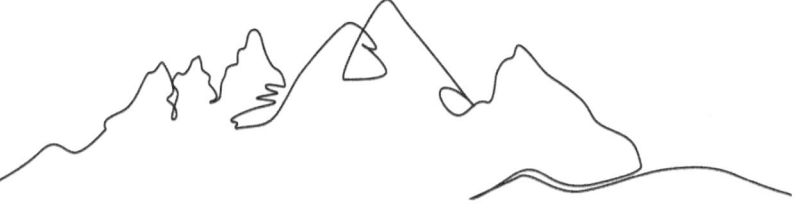

earth is thrown into disarray
all limbs withered
double-jointed roots weave, fight
push naked in the midnight air
the heartbeat remains strong
where mountains embrace

two thousand steps

chatting tongues fold away
boots start to walk in silence
towards the mountain Sanctuary
to say goodbye to the old man
we fell inside way back then
and still, we fall
into poems, songs, his pocket of trinkets
musical wood strapped to our backs
I stop to drink his shadow
cloaked in a giant coast-redwood tree
where hangs a cracked macrocarpa sign
engraved in yellow text
an anthem by Leonard Cohen
"Ring the bells that still can ring
forget the perfect offering
there's a crack, a crack in everything
that's how the light gets in."

we, whānau (family), and I climb the log bridge
the hand-smooth tea tree balustrade
sunlight brushstrokes silver ferns
brown blowfly steals and returns the silence
smudging the air with a whiff of death

white, red, green, and yellow Tibetan prayer flags
fade from neon to weathered wispy grey
someone's guitar string snaps
moss-haired stones spiral

around an ancient gnarley Puriri tree
named Taketakerau;
it shares its birthday with Jesus Christ
its hollow trunk a burial chest
cradling the bones of the Upokorehe Iwi (tribe)
terracotta Buddha sits cross-legged at its base
smiling at each new dawn

petrichor (a scent from the blood of stone)
drifts from the damp earth into the afternoon sun
baby totara tree pushes through a fallen log
Pohutukawa trees blossom
in crimson bottle brushes
yellow striped bumblebees' sizzle
over butter and egg yolk flowers
the azure sky and cumulus clouds
break through a hole in the green
a distant church bell rings
we forget our perfect offering
listen as my foot cracks a new fallen twig

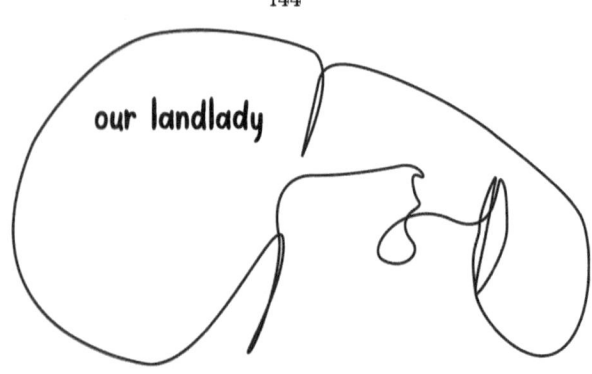

our landlady

is the only known planet
to harbour life, she asks for no rent
as she spirals the daily sun
delivering clean air, water
to billions of passengers
she whispers world music into ears
her tenants do not hear
atom by atom, cell by cell
mother organizes without organizing
takes no counsel with historians
museums, shareholders, churches
only the company of the universe
water wells, fire feasts
earth erupts and wind whips
no rest in rusting, peace is her sleep
her planet rotates
she cloaks man
in a veil of darkness
leaving him digging
for light

colonial mask

I sit on top of mount Rangihoua
Waiheke Island's 360-degree lookout
spans from sky city
to Great Barrier Island
the contour of the island is a dragon
sleeping in green and turquoise waters
cumulus clouds gather grey
and white, hijacking the blue sky
biting winds whip spikey tussock grass
a black-tar sealed road escapes
the chaos
winding its way through thick bush
down to the sea birds
of Whakanewha park
distant rural fields glow amber
sun's rays struggle
to break-through
in sporting shades of green
golf course, tennis court, soccer, rugby fields
harbour ant-like people as they kick
a white speck
between matchstick goalposts
yellow helicopter pads lie like square Lego eyes
rusty red and green vineyards
stripe and march neat lines
onto the country landscape
sea channels it's way inland
sipping up mangrove wetlands

passing colourful houseboats
hidden amongst the tea tree and kahikatea
standing on a rock
at the peak of the mountain
a German woman, brown hair blowing
sings and chants in Maori
her wailing voice slices the wind
and her steel arms cut the air
pointing east, west, north, south
'wild wind blow the stars
spritsails flap to the meeting place
at the great Hawaiki, Hawaiki
to the waters of the Waitemata
turn in to the sacred mountains
of Tamaki Makaurau'

we have stood here before

although I cannot remember when
leaning forward
gently pressing
noses and foreheads together
sharing the same breath
the first tap, us
second, our ancestors
hands grip
you lay your left on my shoulder
brown eyes drill
into the soil of my aorta

Maori and Pakeha
a green Koru fern frond spirals
the outer coil a vortex
of perpetual movement
its inner coil returns
to the same point of origin
the brow, love and honour
the eyebrows, a bird's wingspan
and the tail of the whale
the nose, the body of the whale
eye to seeing eye
link in and remember
part of the same oneness
of everything that exists
blown by strange winds
my heartbeat races
we have stood here before
cannot remember when

golden hour

a yellow sun cuts center stage
light scatters and jives
through invisible air particles
colours mute and muddy the sky
swirl and collide
saturated and visceral
the sun explodes, a lamp in foggy clouds
Tuscan sin burns to butterscotch
a bloated orange morphs into an apricot
melting into the sea
fire exalts into gold
the ocean pulls
  up her lake-blue pyjamas
      as a staircase of waves
            ripples in pink and purple
                stripes, from the horizon
                    to the peninsula I stand
water laps and licks the rocks beneath
oystercatcher, kingfisher, tui
call tintinnabulation to the day's farewell
behind me, a giant Pohutukawa tree
lifts her skirt to curtsy the goldenrod of the sun
her trunk and branches illuminated
as a million green leaves look down to say
'oh my
        oh my
            I do have legs!'

Kiwi

our brown island bird
flightless and colour-blind
muscular legs dance the bush nightlife
taloned footprints kiss up the quiet earth
as Aotearoa sleeps
inside his fluffy smile

ouzo at my table

a blonde holds her windswept hair
with her right-hand she paints
a watercolor horse, another blonde
(platinum and honey)
could be her German mother
armed in copper and silver bracelets
sips coffee from a cherry bowl
she reads the business section

a slim, hennaed woman
wears scarlet linen
rusty leather backpack sits
an old gentleman with a white beard
wearing rose sunglasses crosses the room
grabbing a napkin
to dry his travel map

'so, so you think you can tell
heaven from hell?
blue skies from pain?
can you tell a green field
from cold steel rain?'

everyone seems to have ordered
walnut pear and rocket salad
sprinkled in parmesan and balsamic
the Italian waitress dressed in black

beams a pearly smile and fills her pockets
the local jazz singer (off duty)
cracks old jokes with her jaws
that shatter onto the slate floor

'do you think you can tell?
two lost souls swimming in a fishbowl
year after year'

I slip into my own body
clouds ouzo from oyster cream
canary yellow melts butterscotch
warm sand cascades out of my fingertips
down my legs and pools over
my smiling feet, under the table

Palm Beach

after a marathon-length service to the machine
held hostage, kidnapped. My fractured family
spills onto the white sand
of a deserted beach
the three of us run naked
feet hammering wet sand
kicking a spray of turquoise sea
beaming faces blind even the sun
as we dive like a romp of otters
into the sparkling water
a flying circus of surging hormones
dopamine, oxytocin, vasopressin fires
up the canons engine brain and body
catapulted out of the grey
the magician's happy spell
hangs its daisy chain, champagne fizz
runs up the back of my neck
to pop my head off
sweet flesh and blood of kin
breathe sun in me again

NZ postcard

this land
of the long white cloud
crafted, packed into this small country
snow-capped peaks, rainforests
deserts coastal glaciers
icy fiords, fish-filled rivers, waterfalls
a landscape camera strapped
to my neck as I fly from north
to south
an ocean
of country, fauna, culture
dawn's yellow sunbeams
illuminate champagne bubbles
swirling in tides on east coast beaches
boiling plopping mud pools
serve morning porridge
for Ruaumoko, the god of volcanoes and
earthquakes
hissing geysers erupt
a fierce Maori haka war dance
foot-stamping, body slapping
wide-eyed Pukana tongue stretching and baring
teeth
brothers tattooed chin ink pride
strength and unity
vast snow-peaked mountains vault
white glaciers, ice walls, hungry crevices
soft rolling green hills peppered

with sheep and bush
the silent kiwi hides
as the cheeky colourful kea prance
the southern coast's shy hector's dolphin
makes way
for the exuberant hooker's sea lion
on the Coromandel beach
my shovel digs a hole in the sand
geothermal hot water rises to lick naked legs
mingling with cold ocean waves
a glass of Mudbrick's velvety red
melts delirious tastebuds
the tide rolls in
at the last stop of the day
white and purple lavender flowers
flood my wooden cottage balcony
green lawn stretches from my island home
amongst the manuka trees in Okoka bay
orange flowering flax-bush
flag the blue and green Tui bird
his white throat tufts and bronze iridescent sheen
mark this New Zealander
warrior of the sky
the tide makes its way
skipping up the salty mudflats
birds make last calls
the triumphant sun melts her lips
over a calm turquoise sea
sunrays cut fanned arms through clouds
of amber and gold
I come home to myself

Acknowledgments

I would like to thank the following for their contributions.

Mike Johnson

For almost two years Mike and I reviewed and edited over 300 poems for this book. Working with Mike was one of my highlights each week. I am honoured to have received his considerable experience as a NZ poet, writer and teacher. His ability to guide and shape me as a poet, without losing a sense of my own voice, was precious to me.

Bas Sharp

Sometimes some one will say something casually, almost as an act of kindness to support you, like when Bas said to me "So when is the poetry book coming out Steve?' His light shone through my armours' crack to plant a seed inside my heart. That was six years ago and that one act of kindness produced this book.

Kerry Wade

Kerry is a creative writer and editor of poetry. She put the final touches on this book and helped me to order the poems. It was so exciting to get her fresh, sharp, perspective from the other side of the world. I am so grateful for Kerry's love of poetry, craftsmanship, clarity, and dedication to the work.

Natalya Klimova

The cover of this book is from a painting called "Expectations" by the talented Russian artist Natalya Klimova. Natalya lives and works in Saint Petersburg. She believes that beauty and art can save our world and that great art can penetrate the soul of the audience better than any words.

Janine Edge

For her tenacious support and guidance whilst navigating me through a long dark tunnel

Tina Sailer

For her consistent and hilarious karate attempts to trip up and land me on my back whilst on long walks at the beach. Forever keeping me in the present and connected to the joy of life.

Stephen Hollins grew up in Auckland's eastern
suburbs. Where, tree huts, horses, and cows
played in the fields. On his first day at school he
dressed up as Zorro. He later followed his father
to become a Master Builder. But to his father's
disappointment, he dyed his hair blue and ran
away with the circus to Melbourne. Where he
worked as a clown, singer, actor, writer/director
and performance artist. He returned to Auckland
in 2000. Teaching physical theatre, improvisation,
and established Living Theatre. He has a Diploma
of Drama from Auckland University (1986) and
has studied theatre at Victoria University. Has
trained and taught at several international theatre
schools. Stephen discovered poetry while walking
the Camino de Santiago trail. He has been writing
with a passion ever since.

www.ingramcontent.com/pod-product-compliance
Lightning Source LLC
Chambersburg PA
CBHW031531120626
46545CB00005B/2103

* 9 7 8 1 9 9 1 1 6 0 5 3 9 *